MIDDLE SCHOOL UNIVERSITY

A Parent's Guide to Educational Success in Grades 6-12

DR. TERESA WILBURN

Disclaimer

The information published in this book represents the opinions, personal research, and business experience of the author. Since the success of anyone depends upon the skill and ability of the person, author makes no guarantees and disclaims any personal loss or liabilities that may occur as a result of the use of the information contained herein.

This publication is designed to provide accurate and authoritative information in regard to the subject matter covered in it. It is provided with the understanding that the publisher is not engaged in rendering legal, accounting, or other professional services. If legal advice or other expert assistance is required, the services of a competent professional person should be sought.

Copyright © 2016 Dr. Teresa Wilburn – drteresawilburn.com

Layout and Design Editor: Meika Louis-Pierre – meikalouispierre.com

Published by Wilburn Consulting LLC

All rights reserved. No part of this work may be reproduced or transmitted in any form by any means, electronic or mechanical, including photocopying, or by any information storage or retrieval system, except as is expressly permitted by the Copyright Act or in writing from Teresa Wilburn.

ISBN-13: 978-0692804490
ISBN-10: 0692804498

ABOUT THE AUTHOR

DR. TERESA WILBURN

A determined, committed professor of life, Dr. Teresa (Dr. T) Wilburn brings a special brand of compassion and enthusiasm to her work as a professional educator. For nearly 30 years, Dr. T has dedicated her life to inspiring and equipping her students with the tools necessary for success.

Integrating her studies with her experiences in life and the classroom, Dr. T has authored a self-help book entitled, *My Life a Bestselling Novel* released in January 2013. This interactive reader is designed to help people reach their full potential.

Dr. Wilburn uses journaling as a teaching and counseling tool for students as young as kindergarten and as sophisticated as Master's level. "Journaling reaches the soul and helps us to be reflective and grow", says Dr. T.

Growing in popularity as a speaker, Dr. T uses her innovative approach to interactive education to empower and equip her students to expand their minds and broaden their thinking.

Her newest initiative, *Middle School University* provides Middle School parents with useful information about how to prepare their adolescents for college. Sessions focus on empowering parents/caregivers to become advocates in student learning and improved student outcomes that ultimately lead to overall academic success.

Dr. T was born in Chicago, Illinois but raised in Atlanta, Georgia by a strong quorum of hard-working women who expected nothing but the very best. The loving instruction from her mother taught her how to live and laugh, but attending Spelman College taught her how to appreciate learning.

Dr. Teresa holds a Bachelor's degree from Spelman College, a Master's degree in Business Administration from National Louis University, a Master's in School Administration from Jones International University, and an Educational Specialist and Doctorate in Psychology from the University of Sarasota.

In addition to her roles as a school counselor and college professor, Dr. T is a co-host on the Miller-on-the-Mic Radio show in Atlanta where she brings the community news and information as an educational consultant. The popularity of her show has grown phenomenally in the past three years.

ABOUT THIS BOOK

This Middle School University workbook offers the following domains:

- ❑ Enhances literacy development that forms strong partnerships between home, school and the community
- ❑ Supports the goal of parental involvement as required under ESEA and Title 1 funding
- ❑ Provides a step-by-step guide to communicating with teachers, counselors and school administrators
- ❑ Involves parents in their child's academic success in the core areas of math, language arts, science and social studies
- ❑ Empowers parents with the tools to assist their child in selecting a college or career
- ❑ Engages parents in the college admissions process
- ❑ Fosters a 21st century partnership in education with both current and new stakeholders

FORWARD

As a professional educator, I spent most of my career as a college counselor and soon realized how overwhelming the college admission process was for the students, parents, teachers and college admission officers. Even though an abundance of information was available for the students and educators, many of the parents were confused and frustrated regarding the process. Most parents want to use their own college experience, only to find that not only has the entrance process changed, but so has the entire "college experience".

This manual provides the missing link for parents. It is a guide to help parents with middle and high school children prepare for life after high school, whether it is college, a technical school or an immediate career experience. The tools in this workbook are designed to help parents understand specifics about their child that will foster success later in life.

Finally, it involves parents in the educational process of their child by equipping them with the information they need to be an asset for a successful academic experience. In other words, when parents know better, they can do a better job of guiding and maintaining the educational process.

Dr. Teresa Wilburn

IMPORTANT RESOURCES

COLLEGE AND CAREER PLANNING

www.elegibilitycenter.org NCAA – Athletes must fill out this form and send transcripts
www.playnaia.org NAIA – Athletes must fill out this form and send transcripts
www.njcaa.org National Junior College Athletic Association
www.bigfuture.collegeboard.org College exploration, comparisons and scholarships
www.bestschools.com Online college programs and more
www.zinch.com College search, admission chances and scholarships
www.cappex.org College search and scholarships
www.commonapp.org Complete multiple applications at one time
www.collegeview.com College search, application process, financial aid & majors
www.collegenet.com College search and scholarships
www.usnews.com/rankings College and university rankings
www.electroniccampus.org College search, financial aid and careers
www.collegeconfidential.com College search, admissions and paying for college
www.peterson.com Guide to colleges and universities
www.collegeweeklive.com College search, scholarships and applications

FINANCIAL AID AND SCHOLARSHIPS

www.fafsa.ed.gov Federal Application for Student Aid
www.studentaid.ed.gov Financial aid explanations
www.finaid.com Scholarships, loans, savings and military aid
www.fastweb.com Scholarship search
www.gocollege.com Scholarships, loans and grants
www.scholarships.com Scholarship search
www.scholarshipsandgrants.us/ - Scholarship search
www.studentscholarships.org Scholarship search, career information and college search
www.thesalliemaefund.org Scholarships for minorities (includes Black college dollars)
www.blackstudents.com Scholarships for Black students
www.maldef.org Scholarship information for Latinos

Middle School University

TEST INFORMATION AND PREP

www.collegeboard.org PSAT, SAT and AP information and dates
www.actstudent.org ACT registration and information and dates
www.princetonreview.com SAT, ACT, PSAT and AP prep
www.asvabpracticetests.com Practice tests for Armed Services Vocational Aptitude Battery
www.khanacademy.org Test prep for standardized tests

ACADEMIC MAJORS

www.careercruising.com Career guidance
www.mymajors.com Majors, careers and schools
www.collegemajors101.com Videos about college majors and careers

CAREER AND EMPLOYMENT PLANNING

www.ajb.dni.us America's job bank and career one stop
www.careerpath.com Career and personality tests and the career builder network
www.onetcenter.org Occupational information network
www.myfuture.com College, career and military search

Middle School University

HAVE YOU VISITED A COLLEGE LATELY?

Remember it's never too late or too early!

———————

Middle School University

6TH GRADE

Get off to a great start.

STEP #1

Teamwork Makes the Dream Work

DEVELOP an academic partnership with your child to begin this success journey. It will require mutual effort from each person to successfully choose the right college and to secure adequate funds to finance a college education.

Visit **www.drteresawilburn.com** for up to date information on summer camps and scholarship deadlines.

NOTES

STEP #2

Develop A Timeline with Your Child

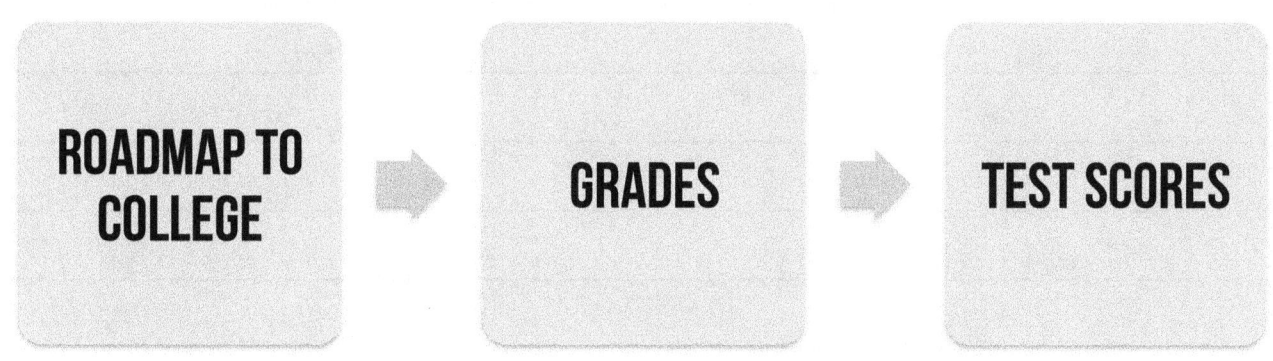

THIS timeline could begin very broadly with a career in mind. Once you narrow down an area of interest, begin analyzing your child's academic and personal strengths and challenges. Review their grades and test scores in the core subject areas including Math, Language Arts, Science and Social Studies. Also, note your child's special interests and talents beyond academics.

NOTES

STEP #3

Knowledge + Action = Power

GATHER all background academic information on your child from your child's school files. This should include current and past grades, test scores, teacher evaluations, etc.

Now that your child has 5-6 years of schooling, this will give you enough information to determine areas of strengths and areas that may present challenges. For example, what are your child's typical grades in Math, Science, Language Arts and Social Studies?

Keep a copy of **ALL** school records and file these documents in a safe place at home or another location.

NOTES

STEP #4

How to Help Your Child in Specific Academic Areas

AS A PARENT...

- ❑ Write your state's educational website here:
  _____

- ❑ Check your state's academic standards in the areas of Math, Science, Social Studies and Language Arts located on the website

- ❑ Determine the standards or goals of each grade in each subject
    - Ex. What should my child know at the end of 6th grade in Math?

- ❑ If your child is having trouble in an academic subject, utilize the state's website for resources in addition to contacting the teacher for recommendations

- ❑ Always look ahead to the next grade level to see what will be expected in the future

- ❑ Your local school district will also share the same information on their website

NOTES

Middle School University

STEP #5

Information You Need to Know

KEEP RECORDS OF...

- ❏ Your child's academic background
- ❏ Grades in all subjects
- ❏ Test scores – standardized as well as informal test data
- ❏ Work samples, projects and teacher's notes (ex. essays, projects, awards and certificates)
- ❏ Honor roll, service tenure, club memberships and athletic records

Visit **www.drteresawilburn.com** for up to date information on summer camps and scholarship deadlines.

NOTES

STEP #6

Where to Get Your Information

MAKE AN APPOINTMENT...

- ❏ Talk with your child's teacher and/or counselor to review details and explanations of report cards
- ❏ Ask school staff to explain the test scores so that you better understand the type of tests given and how your child is performing
- ❏ Ask how you can help your child at home to do better in school. Additionally, secure specific information on websites and other academic tools that your child can access at home

NOTES

STEP #7

Data Collection

YOUR child's teacher is your best source for information, data files and informal records.

- ❏ Talk to the teacher on a regular basis
- ❏ Attend meetings at your scheduled time
- ❏ Understand and respect the classroom environment
- ❏ List your questions for the teacher
- ❏ Keep detailed notes of all meetings
- ❏ Ask how many students are in each class
- ❏ Find out how your child best learns (visual, auditory or experiential)

Your child's score	Your child's percentile
1	1–3
2	4–10
3	11–22
4	23–39
5	40–59
6	60–76
7	77–88
8	89–95
9	96–99

NOTES

STEP #8

Questions to Ask the Teacher

ASK your child's teacher about his/her social skills.

- ❏ Does your child get along well with others?
- ❏ Does he/she present well in front of an audience?
- ❏ What is your child's response to conflict at school?
- ❏ Is your child a leader or a follower?
- ❏ Does the teacher have tips to encourage leadership and self-thinking skills?

Parent/Teacher Conference Notes

Grade_____ Subject/Class _____

Teacher _____ Date _____

Use the back of this page to take notes during your conference.

NOTES

Middle School University

HAVE YOU VISITED A COLLEGE LATELY?

Get in the habit of visiting colleges regularly!

STEP #9

Parent Brag Sheet

DESCRIBE your child- from your point of view - don't be shy! This is a time for your child's light to shine!

- ❑ What does your child do well?
- ❑ What is her/his favorite color?
- ❑ What is her/his favorite animal? season? team?
- ❑ Who are her/his friends?
- ❑ How would you describe her/his personality?
- ❑ What extra-curricular activities are they involved in?
- ❑ What are your child's favorite subjects?
- ❑ Where do they show the greatest strengths?
- ❑ What is your child's learning style?
- ❑ Which techniques motivate your child?
- ❑ What unique awards and honors have they previously earned?

NOTES

STEP #10

Spring Break College Road Trip

WHENEVER you travel around the state or to another state, stop and visit colleges along the way.

- ❏ Get a map (or Google) and find out what colleges you will encounter while traveling
- ❏ It's better to have an appointment, but if you don't, still stop by the campus and take in the sites
- ❏ Pick up a campus newspaper and visit the common area on campus to get a feel for the students and the atmosphere
- ❏ Get a list of the extracurricular activities offered at each college

Visit **www.drteresawilburn.com** for up to date information on summer camps and scholarship deadlines.

NOTES

STEP #11

Review Report Cards and Transcripts

SUMMER, SUMMER, SUMMERTIME!

- ❏ Every summer review your child's report card
- ❏ Take note of academic strengths and weaknesses
- ❏ Focus on the best grades and strengths first, then talk about areas needing improvement
- ❏ Have discussions about the findings and make notes of things to do differently next year to improve
- ❏ Allow time for your child to share his/her feelings, opinions and ideas about their school year
- ❏ Identify and write out specific goals for the next school year
- ❏ Post these goals somewhere visible and review them during the summer

NOTES

STEP #12

Utilize Your Summer

ALLOW YOUR CHILD TO:

- ❏ Get involved in activities that will enhance their overall well-being, including their social skills
- ❏ Explore activities that your school may not sponsor (ex. horseback riding, archery, chess)
- ❏ Search for local camps with indoor and outdoor experiences
- ❏ Take time to visit local junior, private and state colleges in your area.

Who knows, while exploring new activities, your child may enjoy something they never knew existed!

NOTES

STEP #13

Keep Colleges in Mind for Summer Experiences

MOST colleges offer various types of summer programs.

- ❑ Contact colleges near you to see what is available
- ❑ Explore and investigate early. Most deadlines for these programs begin in January and February
- ❑ Consider choosing something different from what you did last summer
- ❑ Keep in mind that colleges love, respect and choose well-rounded applicants
- ❑ This is a time for you to engage in the exploration of activities to expand your child's experiences

Visit **www.drteresawilburn.com** for up to date information on summer camps and scholarship deadlines.

NOTES

STEP #14

Consider These Options

WHAT type of school of higher education is a good fit for your child?

- ❏ A big university: over 10,000 students?
- ❏ A mid-sized college: 5,000 - 10,000 students?
- ❏ A small college: under 5,000 students?
- ❏ A school close to home or far away?

NOTES

STEP #15

Keep a Journal

MAINTAIN a journal of your child's activities, college visits, and adventures. Use the back of this page to list experiences your child has had so far (this book is a good resource).

Visit **www.drteresawilburn.com** for up to date information on summer camps and scholarship deadlines.

NOTES

STEP #16

Academic Challenges: Face Them Early

IF your child faces academic challenges in elementary or middle school, address these academic areas ASAP!

- ❑ Listen carefully to the teacher and take notes
- ❑ Do not ignore suggestions or recommendations given early. Follow through and ask questions as you seek solutions
- ❑ Speak to the school counselor and/or designated administrator for additional available resources
- ❑ Seek a professional second opinion if problems persist
- ❑ Involve and engage your child in this important process
- ❑ Maintain a positive, affirming approach in this process

NOTES

Middle School University

7TH GRADE

Time to get involved in the community.

STEP #17

Utilize Your Summer

THIS is time for you as a parent to make notes of constants in your child. In other words, what remains the same about them (personally, socially and academically) or what has changed?

Pay attention to their behavior, grades, friends, activities, and interests. This information is based on what you have observed.

- ❏ Meet with the teacher and or counselor. Most middle schools have regularly scheduled parent/teacher conferences throughout the school year. Find out when this meeting is set for your 7th grader
- ❏ Attend the meeting (arrive early) and take past report cards and test scores to review and compare
- ❏ Listen! It is always good to hear (the good and the not so good) from your child's teacher. *Take notes!*
- ❏ Always thank the teacher for their work! (This should have been number one!) (SMILE)

NOTES

STEP #18

Get Involved

COLLEGE admissions officers and hiring managers expect students to volunteer their time to give back to the community.

Whether it is helping elderly neighbors by mowing the lawn, babysitting, or joining a well-known organization (i.e. Redcross), get your child INVOLVED!

What extracurricular activities does your middle school offer?
- ❏ Girl Scouts/Boy Scouts
- ❏ Peer leadership
- ❏ Band activities
- ❏ Sports
- ❏ Science Fair
- ❏ Spelling Bee
- ❏ Clubs

NOTES

Middle School University

HAVE YOU VISITED A COLLEGE LATELY?

Get in the habit of visiting colleges regularly!

STEP #19

Call a Local College Admissions Office to Schedule a Campus Visit and Tour

YOU will likely be able to schedule your campus visit online.

While you are on campus:
- ❑ Visit the financial aid office
- ❑ Visit the student center
- ❑ Speak to a professor and/or a dean of education
- ❑ Speak with a coach (if you are in athletics)
- ❑ Visit the gym, the cafeteria, and a classroom, etc.
- ❑ Visit the fine arts center and concert hall
- ❑ Get a copy of the campus newspaper to see what's going on
- ❑ Ask about campus safety and crime statistics
- ❑ Inquire about any summer programs for middle school students
- ❑ Interview students on campus

NOTES

STEP #20

Read and Volunteer

NOW is the time to start gathering information about the college application process and volunteering on a regular basis.

- ❑ Start browsing information about colleges online
- ❑ Get on their mailing lists so they can send you information about scholarships and summer programs
- ❑ Seek out the assistance of a currently enrolled college student to discuss their application process and experiences
- ❑ Find an interesting way to volunteer. Here are a few places to look:
  - Tutor elementary school students in your area
  - Habitat for Humanity
  - Political campaign offices
  - Soup kitchen
  - Your church or place of worship

View additional options at: www.volunteermatch.org

NOTES

STEP #21

Have Your Child Build a Network

KEEP an address book of contacts of people you and your child meet while touring campuses and volunteering. These are professionals who will be able to write letters of recommendation for future work college, and career opportunities.

- ❏ Include their name, email address, phone number and mailing address
- ❏ Periodically send important updates about your child's progress in school and in other activities

NOTES

8TH GRADE

Congratulations!

You made it to the final year of middle school. This year will come and go quickly, therefore there are many tasks and activities for you and your child to keep in mind, review and complete.

STEP #22

Begin the Transition to High School

IT'S time to help your child get organized for success in high school.

- ❑ Review grades from last year and set specific academic and personal goals for this very important year
- ❑ Meet teachers early in the school year
- ❑ Check the school's website regularly for special dates and information for 8th graders

NOTES

STEP #23

Review Carefully

REVIEW all academic information carefully and keep detailed notes about:

- ❏ Past grades in all subjects
- ❏ Test scores both formal (standardized) and informal (teacher created)
- ❏ Report cards and notes from the teacher and counselors
- ❏ Extracurricular activities and special projects

Keep notes on all this information either in your own parent journal or in a safe file. This book is a great resource to record notes and other important documents about your child.

NOTES

STEP #24

Middle School Parent/Teacher Conferences

DURING your individual conferences with your child's teachers:

- ❏ Ask for the teacher's advice on suggestions for high school success strategies
- ❏ Ask the teachers what level of courses your child should take in high school
- ❏ Understand the teacher's rationale for the selection of recommended courses
- ❏ Ask any questions you may have about your child's behavior, level of motivation, and peer interaction

NOTES

STEP #25

Homework and More

TYPICAL DIALOGUE:

Parent: *Do you have any homework?*

Child: *No* - or- Child: *I did it at school.*

How the discussion should go:

Parent: *Let me see your homework.*

Child: *Ok, in Math...Science...Social Studies... Language Arts...*

Note to parents...THERE IS ALWAYS HOMEWORK!

Have a daily routine for homework which includes:

- ❏ A quiet, clear space for your child to study
- ❏ Special time allotted (amount depends on grade level)

Provide resources such as:

- ❏ Pens, pencils and paper
- ❏ Poster boards and art supplies
- ❏ Computer access and a thumb drive

NOTES

STEP #26

Know How Much Time is Recommended for Homework

MINUTES RECOMMENDED EACH DAY:

6th grade - 45-60 minutes

7th grade - 60-75 minutes

8th grade - 60-75 minutes

NOTES

STEP #27

Other Uses for Homework Time

IN addition to any written assignments given by teachers, students should spend time reviewing each subject daily.

- ❑ Reciting or reviewing daily lessons with family members is a great way to reinforce and retain information
- ❑ Always remember to have your child place completed assignments in their book bag at night
- ❑ Many teachers now have drop boxes or email to send assignments
- ❑ Have your child email themselves or you to save assignments
- ❑ Most school districts have online access to many practice standardized tests for FREE
- ❑ Have your child get in the habit of visiting this site and practicing 3-5 questions from this site each day
- ❑ Keep in mind that successful test taking is a SKILL learned through detailed academic strategies
- ❑ The more they practice, the higher their test scores will reflect

Middle School University

NOTES

STEP #28

Preparing for High School

IN January of your child's 8th grade year, conduct an online search for summer programs. These programs could include, but should not be limited to:

- ❏ Volunteer opportunities
- ❏ Internships
- ❏ Academic programs
- ❏ Sports programs
- ❏ On-campus college programs
- ❏ Adventure summer camps
- ❏ Church summer camps

Visit **www.drteresawilburn.com** for up to date information on summer camps and scholarship deadlines.

NOTES

STEP #29

Spring of 8th Grade Year

TO adequately prepare for the forthcoming high school experience:

- ❏ Visit the high school your child is planning to attend (Visit in the fall if you are attending private school)
- ❏ Many high schools have open houses and tours for students and parents. If not, call the school and set up a time to visit
- ❏ Talk to other students and parents who attend these sessions
- ❏ Speak to teachers and coaches about getting your child involved
- ❏ Find out if they offer any academic or sports summer programs as well

NOTES

STEP #30

Planning for Success in High School

AFTER visiting the high school your child is planning to attend, complete these important tasks:

- ❏ Select a 4-year plan of courses (Most schools already have a basic plan. You may only have to assist your child with elective courses.)
- ❏ Contact coaches and/or club sponsors where your child shows interest or has special talents
- ❏ Sign up for club and extracurricular activities
- ❏ Join the PTA and actively volunteer your time and service
- ❏ Modeling leadership in activities is a great way for your child to learn these skills

NOTES

STEP #31

Guidelines for Parents to Follow

FOR your child to be successful in school and beyond, it is necessary for you to be actively involved on a regular schedule.

- ❏ Join the PTA and actively volunteer
- ❏ Sign up to view your child's grades online on Grade Link or Parent Portal. (It is labeled differently in each respective school district.)
- ❏ View your child's grades at least once a week
- ❏ Look for any missing assignments and grades posted by the teacher
- ❏ Set up a weekly conversation with your child regarding the grades posted by teachers
- ❏ Carefully monitor your child's online activities on Facebook, Snap Chat, Twitter, Instagram, etc. Colleges and potential employers review this information

NOTES

STEP #32

Summer Reading List

MOST high schools have a required summer reading list.

- ❑ Check your child's school website for the list or ask the teacher or librarian for suggestions
- ❑ Purchase books or make sure your child has access to the books online
- ❑ Seek assistance from research librarians at any public library
- ❑ Assist your child in making a timeline to complete the summer reading list and related activities
- ❑ Create a simple check off chart or graph to evaluate the reading progress

NOTES

STEP #33

As Soon as Your Child Enters High School, Create a Plan of Action

THE summer before high school begins:

- ❑ Know and understand your child's previous grades and test scores
- ❑ Visit several colleges
- ❑ Allow your child to volunteer for a worthy cause
- ❑ Respond to any and all information received from the high school
- ❑ Make sure your child is involved in some type of summer program/camp
- ❑ Sign up for high school parent online access to grades
- ❑ Visit the high school and learn the layout of the building
- ❑ Review the first-semester academic class schedule
- ❑ Set up selected and appropriate activities for community service hours

NOTES

Middle School University

9TH GRADE

Welcome to High School!

STEP #34

At the Beginning of High School

BEGIN the high school journey on the right foot by getting involved immediately.

- ❏ Attend freshman night for parents
- ❏ Meet all of your child's teachers
- ❏ Get copies of syllabi or course guides (Many teachers have these posted online so you can download and review each with your child.)
- ❏ Note and record on a calendar all special projects or books to be read during the semester
- ❏ Walk through your child's schedule, find the locker and practice how to easily open it
- ❏ Sign up for a regular and a gym locker if necessary
- ❏ Find out how to access the lunch menu
- ❏ Set up a breakfast and lunch account

NOTES

STEP #35

Check, Check and Double Check

MAKE sure that you and your child are clear regarding what is required for graduation.

- ❏ Know your child's classes
- ❏ Understand the graduation requirements in your state
- ❏ Know the credits required for graduation
- ❏ Learn about special testing requirements (standardized, end-of-course, etc.)
- ❏ If you still have questions, contact your child's counselor or school administrator. In most schools this is the **ASSISTANT** principal for instruction and curriculum
- ❏ Continue and highlight community service activities

NOTES

STEP #36

Extracurricular Activities

FIND out about all the available activities at your new high school.

- ❏ Visit the school's website for clubs and sports
- ❏ Meet coaches and club sponsors during parent night to get details of practices, fees and materials needed
- ❏ Encourage your child to get involved in student government or participate in leadership roles at school
- ❏ Check out tutoring sessions or other special programs designed to promote and enhance achievement
- ❏ Watch for test-taking strategy sessions offered by the school

NOTES

STEP #37

Important Leaders You Should Know at the School

ESTABLISH a relationship with all of the following people at your child's school.

- ❏ Teachers - Your BEST Resource
- ❏ Counselor
- ❏ Assistant Principal
- ❏ PTA-President
- ❏ Coaches
- ❏ Club Sponsors
- ❏ School Resource Officer
- ❏ School Secretary/Clerk
  (Main Office and Counselor's Office)
- ❏ Your child's friends!

NOTES

STEP #38

Start a File on Scholarships

DON'T wait to begin searching for scholarships. The time is now!

- ❏ Start searching for college scholarships online
- ❏ Take note of GPA and other requirements
- ❏ Enhance community volunteer opportunities for your child (At church, in your neighborhood, local politics, etc.)
- ❏ Network with other parents who are in search of scholarship funds
- ❏ Many top colleges rate the level of a student's volunteerism very high. It may be used as an entrance tie-breaker

NOTES

STEP #39

More About 9th Grade

MAKE sure you follow up on each of these points so that you are fully aware of where your child stands academically.

- ❑ Carefully review your child's grade at the end of each semester
- ❑ Pay special attention to the number of credits earned each semester and the GPA calculation
- ❑ Know the difference between your child's CORE and Cumulative GPA
- ❑ Hold special conversations with your child on his/her thoughts, wishes, dislikes and interests at school
- ❑ Attend regularly scheduled conferences with your child's teacher

NOTES

STEP #40

Summer After 9th Grade

USE the summer months to get a jump start on 10th grade.

- ❑ Prepare for 10th grade summer reading
- ❑ Continue volunteer experiences
- ❑ Participate in summer programs
- ❑ Secure study guides for ACT www.act.org and/or PSAT www.collegeboard.org
- ❑ Have your child take practice tests online in small increments

Special note: Superior test-taking skills are learned! Therefore, knowledgeable study and practice of these skills enhance standardized test scores!

NOTES

Middle School University

HAVE YOU VISITED A COLLEGE LATELY?

Meet a College Admissions Officer!

Middle School University

10TH GRADE

Congratulations, you're a Sophomore!

STEP #41

The Start of Sophomore Year

REGISTER for the PSAT (Practice for the SAT) if your child's school offers it to 10th graders.

- ❏ Review the scores and practice areas that need improvement
- ❏ If your child's school does not offer the PSAT for sophomores, complete 2 practice questions daily. Work through one math and one vocabulary or reading question per day. There are many online resources to practice
- ❏ Check out my website: www.drteresawilburn.com for the SAT vocabulary word of the day

NOTES

STEP #42

Getting Organized for 10th Grade

NARROW down the activities your child may want to pursue in college.

- ❑ Review and revise the goals of college and career choices that correlate to your child's interests and abilities
- ❑ Have your child "job shadow" a person in the field of her/his interest
- ❑ Check with your school counselor for any special programs for sophomores, for example, HOBY (Hugh O'Brien Youth Leadership summer program)
- ❑ Look at churches and places of worship as they often offer many volunteer activities

NOTES

STEP #43

Tips to Remember

CONTINUE and expand all activities started in 9th grade.

- ❏ Find leadership opportunities to enhance growth and development
- ❏ Review any essays your child writes for classes
- ❏ Writing will be a critical part of the college application and scholarship process
- ❏ Identify your child's academic strengths and areas where improvement is needed
- ❏ Talk to teachers to find how to improve areas recognized as needing improvement

NOTES

STEP #44

Mail and Marketers

COLLEGES will begin to send your child loads of mail during the sophomore year.

- ❑ Help your child keep an organized file of mail received
- ❑ Beware of marketers and scammers. Do not pay for programs that congratulate your child with a certificate and require costs to participate
- ❑ Your child's name and address are on several mailing lists because of their activities and grades

NOTES

STEP #45

Be Realistic About Your Child's Grades

ONCE again, prepare for summer. Many colleges offer on-campus programs for rising juniors.

- ❑ Check with colleges that you and your our child visited to determine what they have to offer
- ❑ Monitor your child's GPA and academic standing
- ❑ Select and base your summer college visits on the preliminary grade point average and test scores your child has currently posted
- ❑ Be realistic! What is your child's GPA at the end of sophomore year? _____ _____
                                           Core   Cumulative
- ❑ Be guided by your child's academic status, special talents and unique personal career interests

NOTES

STEP #46

Tell Your Child to Visit Their Counselor

ENCOURAGE your child to visit with the school counselor to see if there are any special programs or courses offered for juniors and seniors, including:

- ❏ Dual/Joint enrollment
- ❏ AP courses
- ❏ Internships
- ❏ Work study programs
- ❏ Technical/Trade School courses

High School is a good time to explore all of these opportunities and have fun while doing it! (smile)

The suggestion is to encourage **your child** to visit the counselor. This is a step to help them take responsibility for their education and be a self-advocate.

Do not do it for them!

NOTES

Middle School University

HAVE YOU VISITED A COLLEGE LATELY?

What scholarships are available?

_____

STEP #47

Finance Makes Sense

TALK with your child about what you are willing to pay for college and what they need to contribute.

- ❏ To avoid "sticker shock", periodically check the price of tuition at the colleges your child is considering
- ❏ Investigate special scholarships and grants offered by your state and colleges on your child's list
- ❏ Visit the financial aid office during the college tour and ask questions about grants and scholarships

Visit **www.drteresawilburn.com** for up to date information on summer camps and scholarship deadlines.

NOTES

Middle School University

11TH GRADE

A Crucial Year!

STEP #48

A Vital Year: 11th Grade

KNOW and track the number of credits your child has earned toward graduation.

- ❑ Is your child on track to graduate on time? With Honors?
- ❑ Know your child's GPA
- ❑ Keep in mind that junior year is the **final year** to improve grades before it's time to submit college applications
- ❑ Schedule your child to take the SAT during the last semester of junior year
- ❑ Select a successful college student for your child to visit or interview. This could be a friend or relative

NOTES

STEP #49

Tips to Remember for 11th Grade

MAKE sure your child registers to take the PSAT in the fall of their junior year.

- ❏ Compare scores with admissions standards of colleges that your child has been researching
- ❏ Attend multiple college fairs **with** your child and apply for summer enrichment programs
- ❏ Find internships and volunteer in a community-based program
- ❏ Assist your child in securing a summer job
- ❏ Create a budget based on the first year of college. Do not wait until senior year to discuss budgeting!

NOTES

Middle School University

HAVE YOU VISITED A COLLEGE LATELY?

What did you like about the campus?
_____

STEP #50

The Big Ten

NARROW DOWN THE COLLEGE APPLICATION PROCESS

College	GPA Req.	SAT/ACT Req.	Programs Offered	Costs	Other
1.					
2.					
3.					
4.					
5.					
6.					
7.					
8.					
9.					
10.					

NOTES

STEP #51

Register to Take the SAT and ACT

IT'S highly suggested that they take one of these tests in the spring of their junior year (March, May or June).

- ❑ Meet with a counselor to schedule senior courses
- ❑ Understand the difference between a weighted and un-weighted GPA
- ❑ Ask a counselor for scholarship suggestions (including local organizations and businesses)
  www.collegeboard.org
  www.act.org

NOTES

STEP #52

College Website Review

VISIT the website(s) of the college where your child is planning to attend and review their financial aid information. Pay special attention to requirements for grants and scholarships offered.

Visit **www.drteresawilburn.com** for up to date information on summer camps and scholarship deadlines.

NOTES

STEP #53

Athletes

IF your child plans to participate in sports during college, they will need to file a registration form with the NCAA as follows:

- ❏ Visit www.ncaa.org
- ❏ Note special GPA and ACT/SAT requirements
- ❏ Meet with coaches for suggestions and networking
- ❏ Attend summer sports programs. (Contact the high school coach for details.)
- ❏ Design and review film highlights from high school
- ❏ Load film on suggested websites provided by coaches
- ❏ Continue training during the summer

NOTES

STEP #54

Dollars and Sense

WHILE visiting colleges, ask specific questions in the financial aid office:

- ❑ What is the total cost to attend including tuition, room, board, additional fees such as labs, travel, books/materials and supplies?
- ❑ Do you require a CSS profile?
- ❑ What is the average financial aid package? Describe the breakdown in grants, scholarships, and loans
- ❑ Does my child qualify for institutionally based scholarships with their current GPA/SAT score?
- ❑ Be realistic! What is your child's GPA at the end of junior year? _____ _____
                                    Core   Cumulative

- ❑ SAT scores   Math_____   Verbal_____

NOTES

Middle School University

STEP #55

Reminders for 11th Grade

GET two copies of your child's updated transcript noting the Grade Point Average on it.

- ❑ Discuss narrowing down your child's college choices
- ❑ Pay careful attention to application fees
- ❑ Start applying for scholarships
- ❑ Make a calendar of admissions and scholarship deadlines
- ❑ Have your child register to take the fall SAT senior year

NOTES

STEP #56

Notes

SUMMARIZE your thoughts and ideas about your child's academic success at this point! Be honest, and chart your course of action moving forward.

_____
_____
_____
_____
_____
_____
_____
_____
_____
_____
_____
_____
_____
_____
_____
_____
_____

Middle School University

HAVE YOU VISITED A COLLEGE LATELY?

Meet a college admissions officer!

STEP #57

Meet a College Admissions Officer

ASK if your child is taking the correct high school classes to meet their entrance requirements. Make changes in their schedule if necessary.

NOTES

STEP #58

Find Summer College Programs

CHECK with select colleges to see if they have summer programs for high school students. These programs can range from sports to academics. The important piece is to expose your child to as many college opportunities as possible. This will give you additional information on their preference and more information about the college.

- ❑ Colleges and universities normally keep students on their mailing lists if they have attended programs on the campus
- ❑ Spend your summer completing and reviewing college applications and essays

Visit **www.drteresawilburn.com** for up to date information on summer camps and scholarship deadlines.

NOTES

Middle School University

12TH GRADE

Yay! You're a Senior!

STEP #59

Senior Year

YOU can now start applying to the colleges you have chosen!

- ❏ Spend time this summer reviewing college applications to see what is required
- ❏ This could include essays and interviews
- ❏ Make a final visit to the campus, just to make sure this a place your child could call home for the next 4 or more years of their lives
- ❏ Register for the first ACT/SAT in the fall

NOTES

STEP #60

Show Me the Money

FILL out as many scholarship and grant applications during the summer as you can. Check the following websites:

- ❑ www.drteresawilburn.com
- ❑ www.fastweb.com
- ❑ www.scholly.com
- ❑ www.uncf.org

Always check the website of the college you are applying to for specific scholarships and grants awarded from the school.

NOTES

STEP #61

Fall of Senior Year

CHECK the early application deadlines of the schools of your choice.

- ❏ Submit all applications as early as possible
- ❏ Note the difference between **early action** and **early decision** for each college on our child's list
- ❏ Stay focused and APPLY ON TIME

NOTES

STEP #62

Reminders for Senior Year

IT is important to know that colleges can always resend any prior admission decisions made if you do not hold you up your end of the deal. (In other words, maintain grades during senior year.)

- ❏ Keep your child focused on current grades
- ❏ This includes staying out of discipline trouble and maintaining grades as they were when your child applied and/or was accepted for admission

NOTES

STEP #63

Accepted

ONCE your child has received an acceptance letter, you can start making preparations for the next move - college life!

- ❑ If your child will stay on campus, make sure you send in the housing deposit early! This deadline will be noted in the acceptance package
- ❑ If your child is staying at home, consider other resources and materials needed for daily transportation to and from the campus as well as updated computers and/or software

NOTES